How to Draw People

50 Learn to Draw

50 People, From Astronaut, Firefighter To Superhero, With These Step-By-Step Guides for Kids!

How to Draw People

Learn To Draw 50 People, From Astronaut, Firefighter To Superhero, With These Step-By-Step Guides for Kids!

This Book Belongs to:

_____

_____

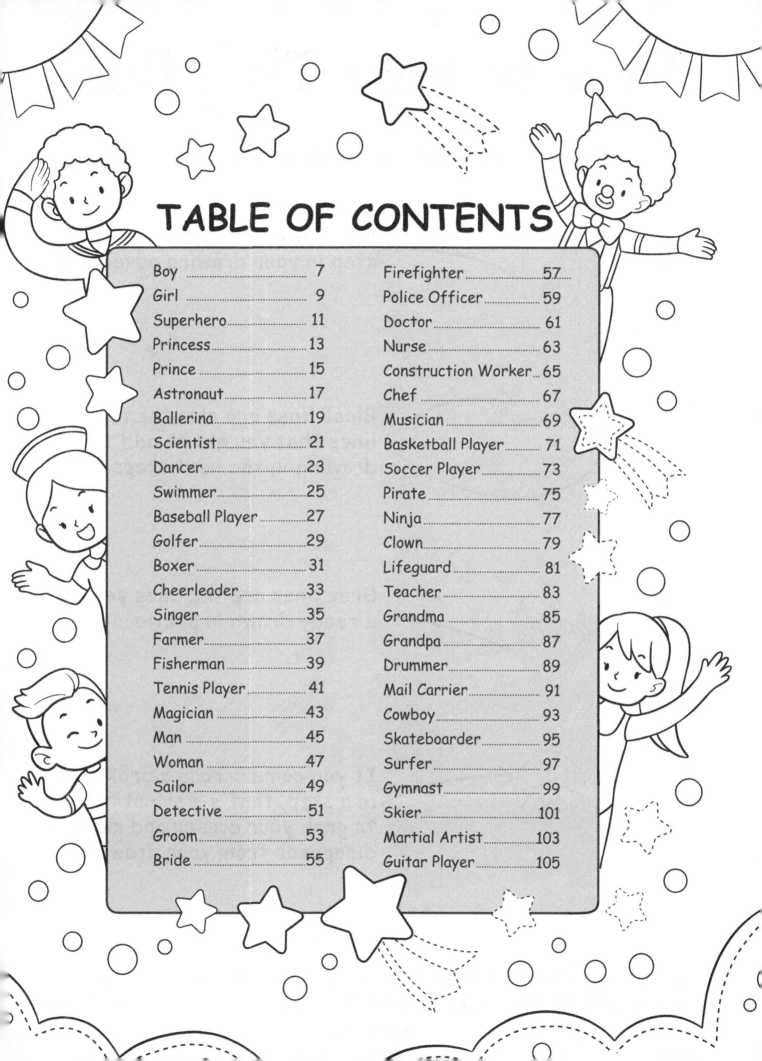

TABLE OF CONTENTS

How to Use This Book

Let's talk about the black lines and gray lines in our guide.

1

Black lines are the start of each step in your drawing adventure!

2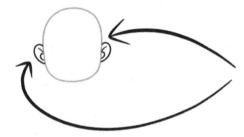

Black lines are also the new lines that you get to add to your drawing in the next steps.

3

Grey lines are the lines you've already drawn in previous steps.

4

If you come across a broken line in a step, that's a signal for you to grab your eraser and make it disappear from your drawing.

Remember, the most important thing is to have fun and enjoy the process! Keep practicing and you'll be creating amazing drawings in no time!

Learn to Draw People

Boy

10

11

12

Let me be your guide,
trace and improve.

Let's use this space to practice our
drawing and improve your skills!

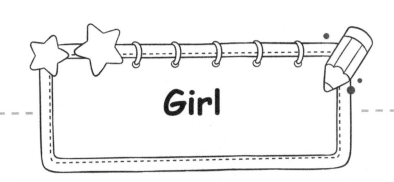

Girl

1

2

3

4

5

6

7

8

9

10

11

12

Follow my lines and bring me to life!

Let's get your pencils ready and practice drawing at this spot!

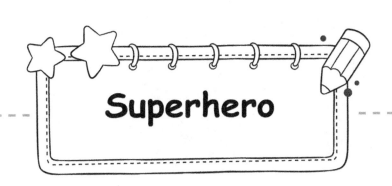

Superhero

1

2

3

4

5

6

7

8

9

11 Superhero

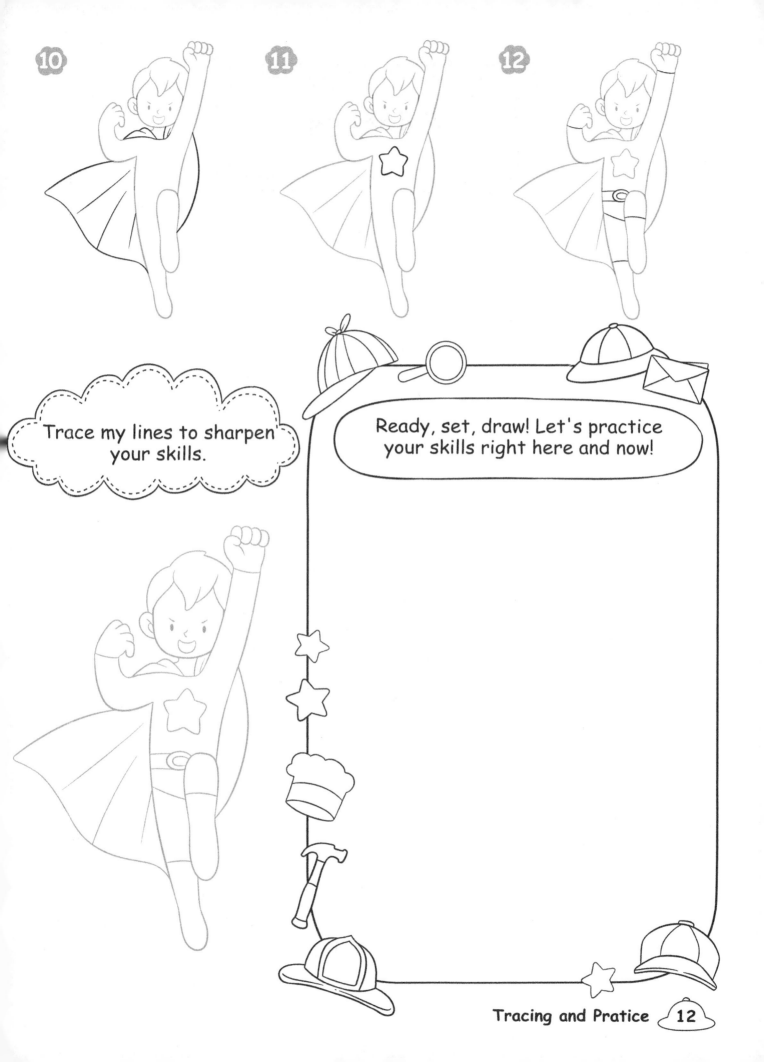

10

11

12

Trace my lines to sharpen your skills.

Ready, set, draw! Let's practice your skills right here and now!

Princess

Follow my outline for a tracing challenge.

It's time to show off our drawing skills! Let's practice at this place!

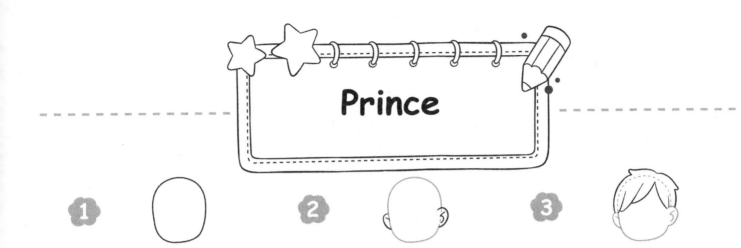

Prince

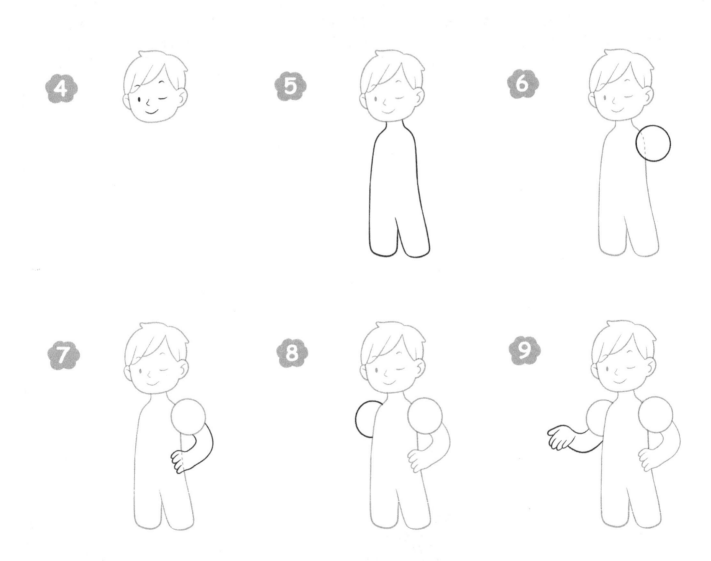

10

11

12

Hone your skills with a trace of me.

Ready to have some fun and practice drawing? Let's do it here!

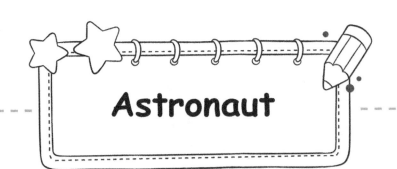

Astronaut

1

2

3

4

5

6

7

8

9

Let me be your guide, trace and improve.

Get your pencils ready, it's time to practice drawing here!

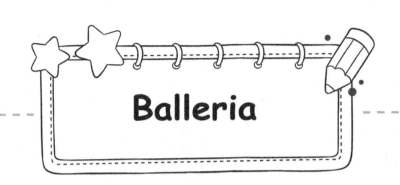

Balleria

1

2

3

4

5

6

7

8

9

10

11

12

Follow my lines and bring me to life!

Let's have some fun and practice our drawing skills here!

Scientist

 1

 2

 3

4

5

 6

7

 8

 9

Trace my lines to sharpen your skills.

Let's use this space to practice our drawing and improve your skills!

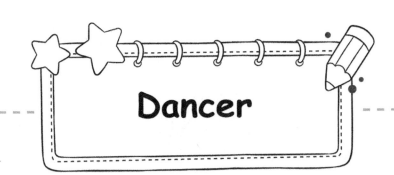

Dancer

1

2

3

4

5

6

7

8

9

10

11

12

Follow my outline for a tracing challenge.

Let's get your pencils ready and practice drawing at this spot!

Swimmer

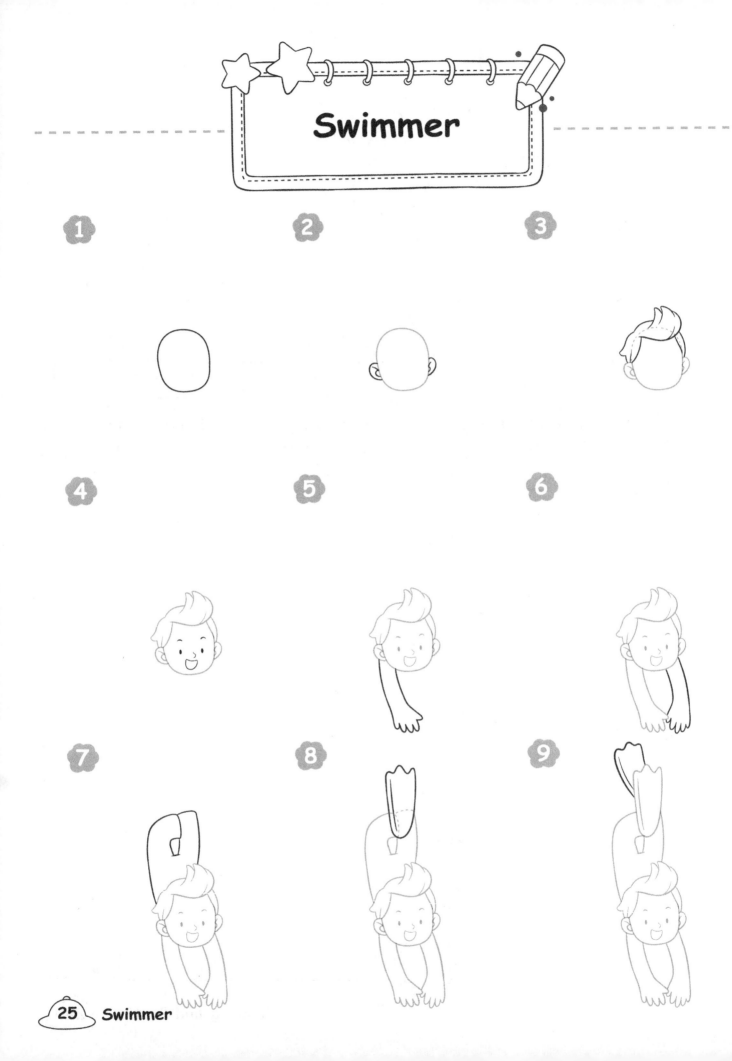

1

2

3

4

5

6

7

8

9

10

11

12

Hone your skills with a trace of me.

Ready, set, draw! Let's practice your skills right here and now!

Baseball Player

1

2

3

4

5

6

7

8

9

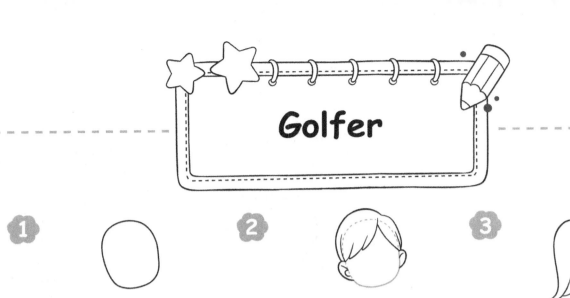

Golfer

10

11

12

Follow my lines and bring me to life!

Ready to have some fun and practice drawing? Let's do it here!

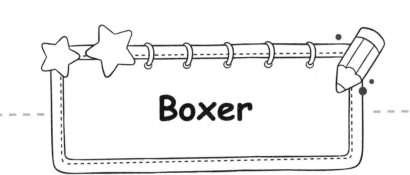

Boxer

1

2

3

4

5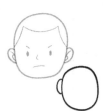

6

7

8

9

Trace my lines to sharpen your skills.

Get your pencils ready, it's time to practice drawing here!

Cheerleader

1

2

3

4

5

6

7

8

9

10

11

12

Follow my outline for a tracing challenge.

Let's have some fun and practice our drawing skills here!

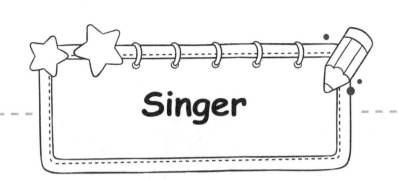

Singer

1

2

3

4

5

6

7

8

9

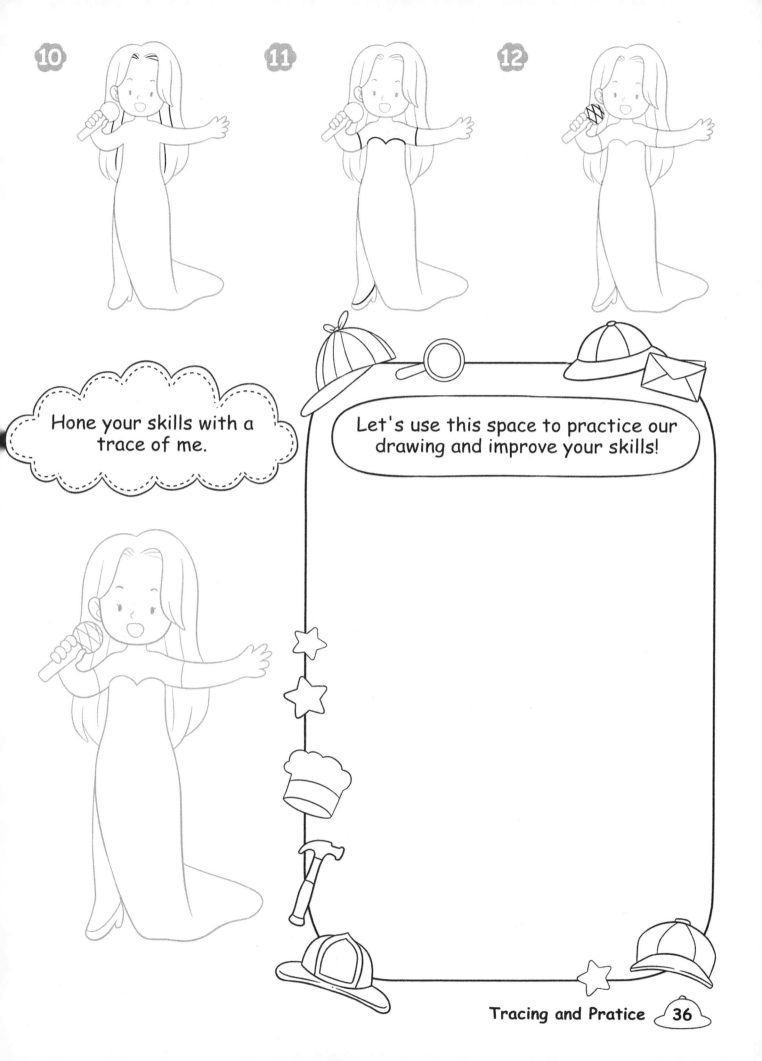

10

11

12

Hone your skills with a trace of me.

Let's use this space to practice our drawing and improve your skills!

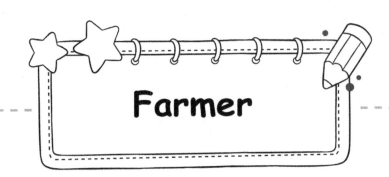

Farmer

1

2

3

4

5

6

7

8

9

Let me be your guide, trace and improve.

Let's get your pencils ready and practice drawing at this spot!

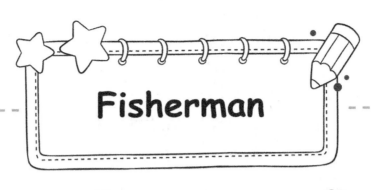

Fisherman

1

2

3

4

5

6

7

8

9

Follow my lines and bring me to life!

Ready, set, draw! Let's practice your skills right here and now!

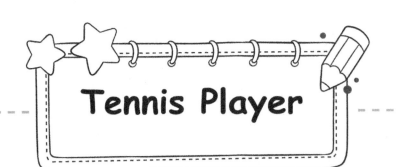

Tennis Player

1

2

3

4

5

6

7

8

9

10 **11** **12**

Trace my lines to sharpen your skills.

It's time to show off our drawing skills! Let's practice at this place!

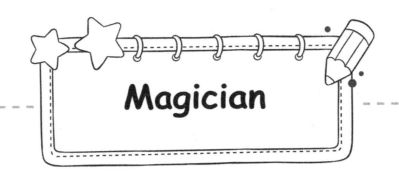

Magician

1

2

3

4

5

6

7

8

9

10

11

12

Follow my outline for a tracing challenge.

Ready to have some fun and practice drawing? Let's do it here!

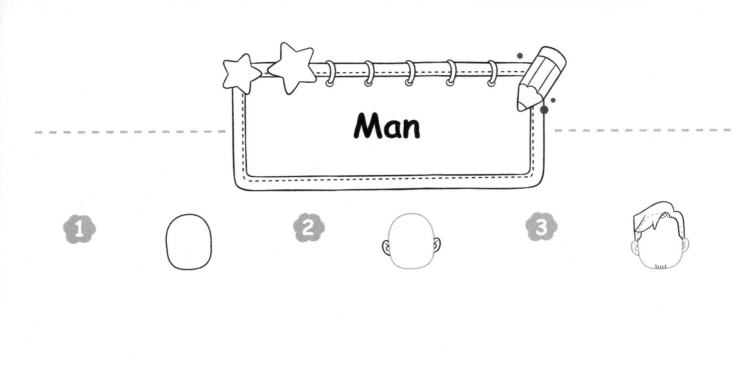

Man

10

11

12

Hone your skills with a trace of me.

Get your pencils ready, it's time to practice drawing here!

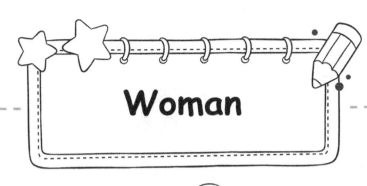

Woman

1

2

3

4

5

6

7

8

9

10

11

12

Let me be your guide, trace and improve.

Let's have some fun and practice our drawing skills here!

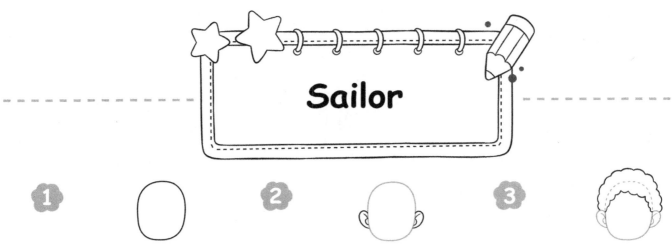

Sailor

Follow my lines and bring me to life!

Let's use this space to practice our drawing and improve your skills!

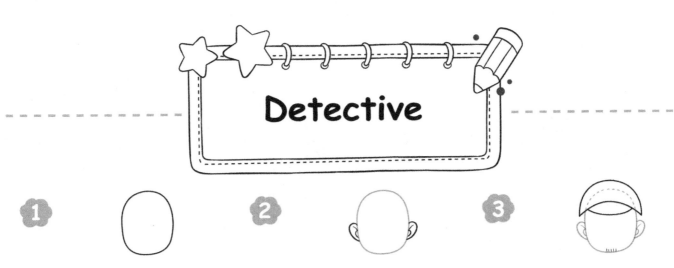

Detective

Trace my lines to sharpen your skills.

Let's get your pencils ready and practice drawing at this spot!

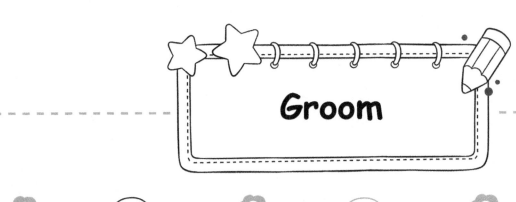

Groom

1

2

3

4

5

6

7

8

9

10

11

12

Follow my outline for a tracing challenge.

Ready, set, draw! Let's practice your skills right here and now!

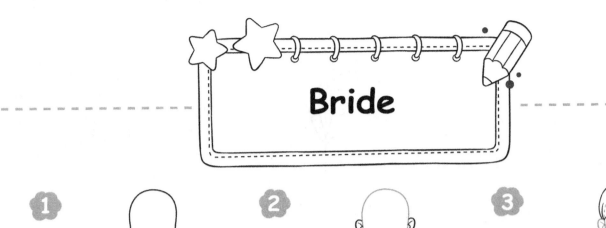

Bride

1

2

3

4

5

6

7

8

9

10

11

12

Hone your skills with a trace of me.

It's time to show off our drawing skills! Let's practice at this place!

Firefighter

1

2

3

4

5

6

7

8

9

10

11

12

Let me be your guide, trace and improve.

Ready to have some fun and practice drawing? Let's do it here!

Police Officer

1

2

3

4

5

6

7

8

9

Follow my lines and bring me to life!

Let's have some fun and practice our drawing skills here!

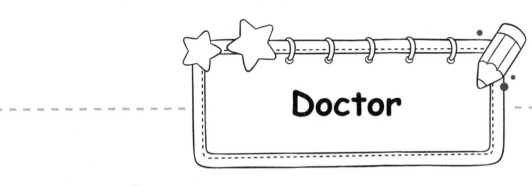

Doctor

1

2

3

4

5

6

7

8

9

Trace my lines to sharpen your skills.

Let's use this space to practice our drawing and improve your skills!

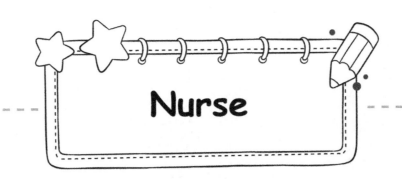

Nurse

1

2

3

4

5

6

7

8

9

Follow my outline for a tracing challenge.

Let's get your pencils ready and practice drawing at this spot!

Construction
Worker

1

2

3

4

5

6

7

8

9

10

11

12

Let me be your guide, trace and improve.

It's time to show off our drawing skills! Let's practice at this place!

Chef

1

2

3

4

5

6

7

8

9

10

11

12

Hone your skills with a trace of me.

Ready, set, draw! Let's practice your skills right here and now!

Musician

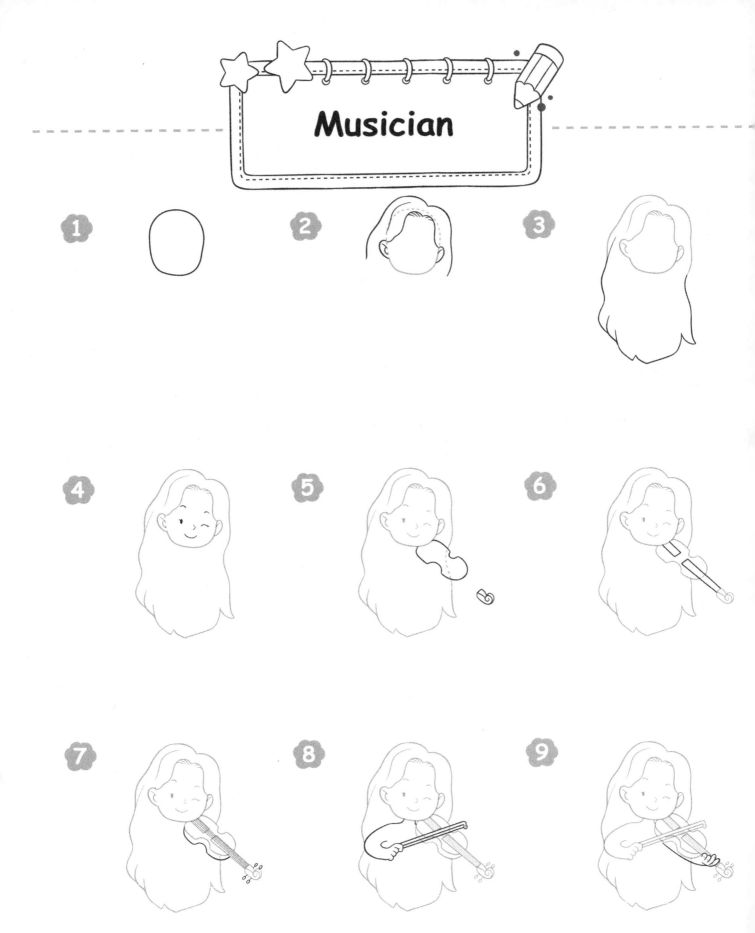

Follow my lines and bring me to life!

Ready to have some fun and practice drawing? Let's do it here!

Basketball player

1

2

3

4

5

6

7

8

9

Trace my lines to sharpen your skills.

Let's have some fun and practice our drawing skills here!

Soccer player

1

2

3

4

5

6

7

8

9

Follow my outline for a tracing challenge.

Let's use this space to practice our drawing and improve your skills!

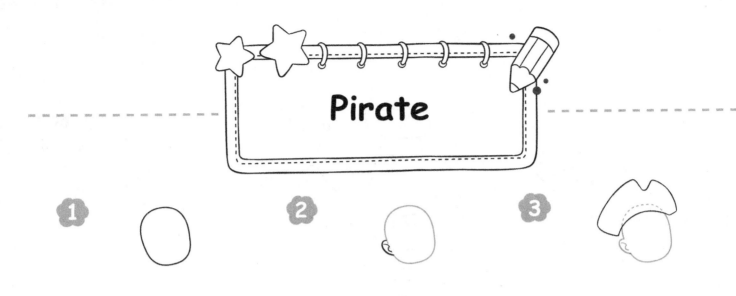

Pirate

1 **2** **3**

4 **5** **6**

7 **8** **9**

10 11 12

Hone your skills with a trace of me.

Let's get your pencils ready and practice drawing at this spot!

Ninja

Let me be your guide, trace and improve.

It's time to show off our drawing skills! Let's practice at this place!

Clown

Follow my lines and bring me to life!

Ready to have some fun and practice drawing? Let's do it here!

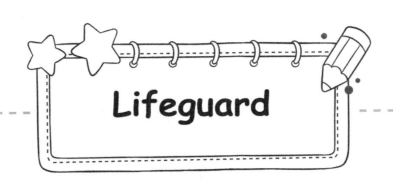

Lifeguard

1

2

3

4

5

6

7

8

9

10

11

12

Trace my lines to sharpen your skills.

Let's have some fun and practice our drawing skills here!

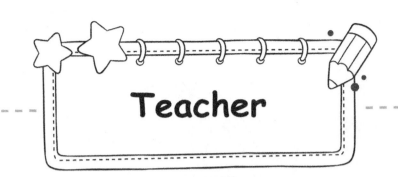

Teacher

1

2

3

4

5

6

7

8

9

Follow my outline for a tracing challenge.

Let's use this space to practice our drawing and improve your skills!

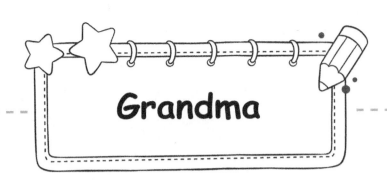

Grandma

1

2

3

4

5

6

7

8

9

10

11

12

Hone your skills with a trace of me.

Let's get your pencils ready and practice drawing at this spot!

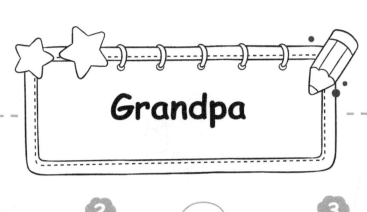

Grandpa

1

2

3

4

5

6

7

8

9

Let me be your guide, trace and improve.

It's time to show off our drawing skills! Let's practice at this place!

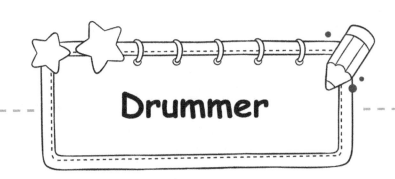

1

2

3

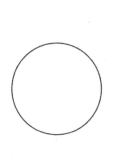

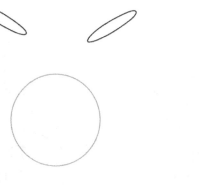

4

5

6

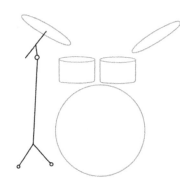

7

8

9

Follow my lines and bring me to life!

Ready to have some fun and practice drawing? Let's do it here!

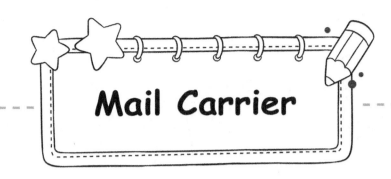

Mail Carrier

1

2

3

4

5

6

7

8

9

Trace my lines to sharpen your skills.

Let's have some fun and practice our drawing skills here!

Cowboy

1

2

3

4

5

6

7

8

9

10

11

12

Follow my outline for a tracing challenge.

Let's use this space to practice our drawing and improve your skills!

Skateboarder

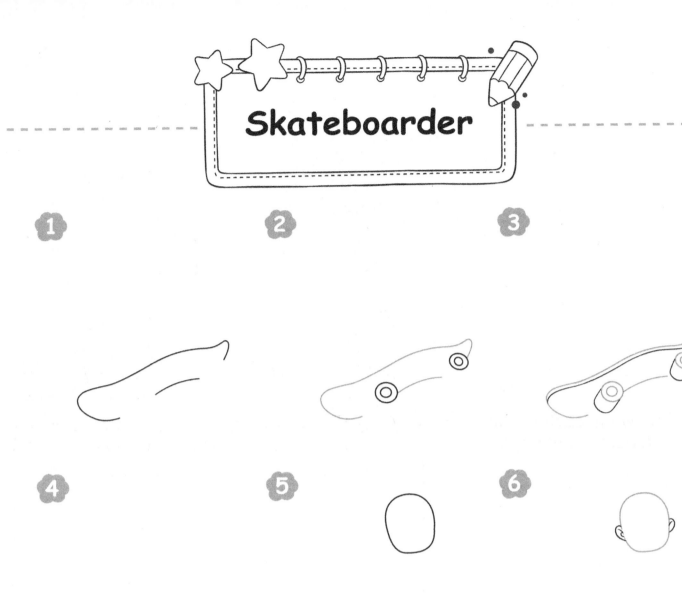

1

2

3

4

5

6

7

8

9

10

11

12

Hone your skills with a trace of me.

Let's get your pencils ready and practice drawing at this spot!

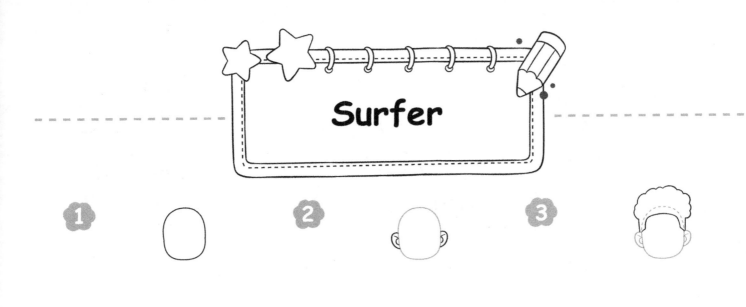

Surfer

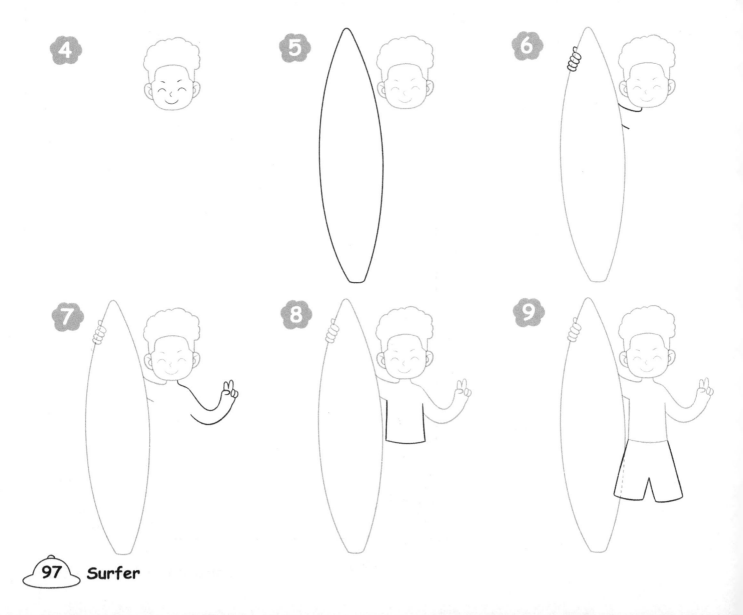

10 **11** **12**

Let me be your guide, trace and improve.

It's time to show off our drawing skills! Let's practice at this place!

Gymnast

1

2

3

4

5

6

7

8

9

10

11

12

Follow my lines and bring me to life!

Ready to have some fun and practice drawing? Let's do it here!

Skier

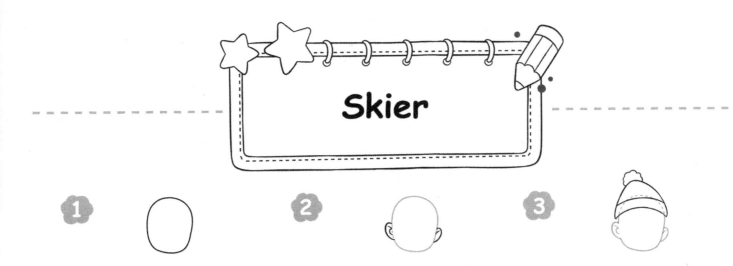

10

11

12

Trace my lines to sharpen your skills.

Let's have some fun and practice our drawing skills here!

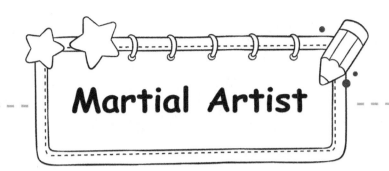

Martial Artist

1

2

3

4

5

6

7

8

9

10

11

12

Follow my outline for a tracing challenge.

Let's use this space to practice our drawing and improve your skills!

Guitar Player

1

2

3

4

5

6

7

8

9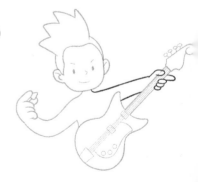

10

11

12

Hone your skills with a trace of me.

Let's get your pencils ready and practice drawing at this spot!

Congratulations, little artist!

You have completed the epic journey of learning how to draw people! We are so proud of you for your hard work and dedication.

Keep practicing and exploring your creativity. Who knows, you might become the next famous artist or illustrator! Remember, the more you practice, the better you will become. Keep up the fantastic work, and keep on drawing!

Made in the USA
Las Vegas, NV
23 December 2024

15283403R00063